ONE MILLION INSECTS

Written by Isabel Thomas

Illustrated by Lou Baker-Smith

WELBECK
EDITIONS

First published in hardback 2021 by Welbeck Editions
This paperback edition published in 2023 by Welbeck Editions
An Imprint of Welbeck Children's Limited, part of Welbeck Publishing Group.
Offices in: London - 20 Mortimer Street, London W1T 3JW
Sydney - 205 Commonwealth Street, Surry Hills 2010
www.welbeckpublishing.com

Design Manager: Emily Clarke
Designer: Miranda Snow
Associate Publisher: Laura Knowles
Editor: Jenni Lazell

A CIP record for this book is available from the Library of Congress.

ISBN 978-1-80338-182-4

Printed in Heshan, China

10 9 8 7 6 5 4 3 2 1

FSC
www.fsc.org
MIX
Paper from
responsible sources
FSC® C020056

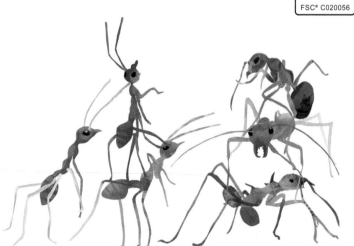

Contents

Welcome to Planet Insect!

Who rules the world? Is it the most numerous animals? Or the group with the greatest number of species? Or the animals that live on all seven continents? Insects are all three!

The first insects appeared around 400 million years ago, long before the time of the dinosaurs. They survived four mass extinctions that wiped out bigger, tougher animals. They watched as mammals and flowering plants appeared for the first time. Right now, up to 10 quintillion insects are creeping, crawling, fluttering, and scuttling in every corner of the world. They outnumber humans by around 1.4 billion to one! Insects are also the most diverse group of living things. Just over a million species have been spotted and named so far.

From the wettest forest to the driest desert, from the frozen Arctic to the tropical rain forest, insects have found ways to survive in every possible habitat. There are even insects that live inside other insects! The million or more species of insects have many differences, but they all share features that make this group so successful.

small size

wings

waxy covering

six legs

Insects aren't just the most successful creatures on the planet—they're also the most important. On these pages you'll meet insects that pollinate plants and spread seeds; insects that prey on pests and provide food for millions of different animals; and insect decomposers, who break down dung and dead things, recycling their particles to be used by new life. One million insects that support almost every ecosystem on Earth.

Is it an insect?

Lift a fallen log, dip a net into a pond, or shake a tree and you'll find our planet is crawling with small animals! But not all of these are insects. What makes insects different—and special?

There are millions of different types of living things on Earth. To keep a track of them, scientists sort them into groups based on their similarities. Insects belong to a large group of animals known as invertebrates—animals without a backbone. In fact, they have no skeleton inside at all. Some invertebrates are squishy as a result, but one group—the arthropods—have a tough covering called an exoskeleton on the outside instead.

This exoskeleton is extremely useful. It provides protection from predators, and it keeps water from coming out of an arthropod's body so it doesn't dry out! All arthropods all have a symmetrical body divided into segments, as well as legs that grow in pairs. Spiders, crabs, and centipedes all share these features, but the biggest group of arthropods is the insects.

Three parts
Each part of an insect's body has a different role. The head has parts for feeding and sensing. The thorax is where the legs and wings are attached. The abdomen contains parts for digesting food and for reproducing.

Winged visitors
Most insects have wings for at least part of their life. They were the first creatures on Earth to ever take to the air. Insects are still the only animals with proper wings that aren't just reshaped arms or fins.

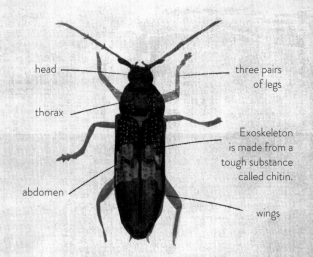

Class: Insects
Species: more than one million
Lives: almost everywhere

head

thorax

abdomen

three pairs of legs

Exoskeleton is made from a tough substance called chitin.

wings

Walking tripods
As an insect walks or runs, it always keeps three feet on the ground—two on one side and one on the other side. This "tripod gait" helps the insect keep its balance or stick to a surface as it climbs straight up!

Eye, eye

How many eyes does this fly have? Look closely . . .
Wasps, bees, and flies all have five eyes! They include
both types of eyes that insects have.

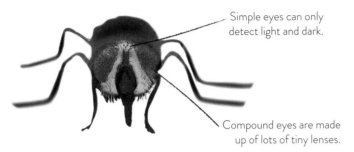

Simple eyes can only
detect light and dark.

Compound eyes are made
up of lots of tiny lenses.

No lungs

Insects breathe air, but not through their mouths or even
their heads. Air gets into their bodies through tiny holes
called spiracles on the sides of their bodies.

Super senses

Senses let an insect find out all about the world around
them, helping them avoid danger, find friends—or find
lunch! Their senses are very different from ours. There are
insects that smell with their antennae, taste with their
feet, hear with their legs, and see with their bottoms!

Flower meals

As insect senses evolved, so
did flowers! Delicious scents
and beautiful colors are
there to tell insects where
to find food. The flowers
advertise free meals of
nectar to ensure they get
pollinated. Some insects
prefer the smell of poop
or dead meat, so there are
flowers that produce those
smells instead!

Spider and scorpion

Arachnids, such as spiders and
scorpions, are arthropods. They have
eight legs and no wings, so they are
not insects.

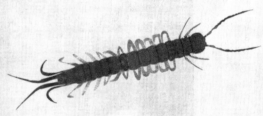

Millipede and centipede

Millipedes and centipedes are arthropods but have
no wings, and they have many more legs and body
segments than insects do.

Pill bugs

Most crustaceans live in water. But pill bugs—also
called wood lice or roly-polies—are crustaceans that
live on land.

Springtails, coneheads, and
two-pronged bristletails

Springtails have six legs, but they never have wings,
their mouthparts are hidden away inside their heads,
and they often don't have eyes or antennae.

Dazzling diversity

Insects are a vast group of animals. The million species we know about have a lot in common but also plenty of weird and wonderful differences.

Insects come in . . .

- all shapes—from long, thin stick insects to large round beetles.
- all sizes—from dinner plate-size moths to fairy wasps too tiny to see.
- all colors—from yellow jackets to peacock butterflies.

Different wings

Most insects have four wings, but some have just one pair, and some never grow wings at all. Insect wings look and work in diverse ways, from the purposely clumsy fluttering butterflies to dragonflies dive-bombing with fighter pilot precision.

Different mouths

An insect's mouthparts give us a big clue about what it likes to eat. Tough jaws are good for chewing leaves or crunching other insects. Needle-sharp tubes are better for piercing skin or stems and sucking blood or sap. A coiled proboscis can find its way to the best-hidden nectar. And sponge-like mouthparts can soak up liquid food—but only if it's been digested beforehand!

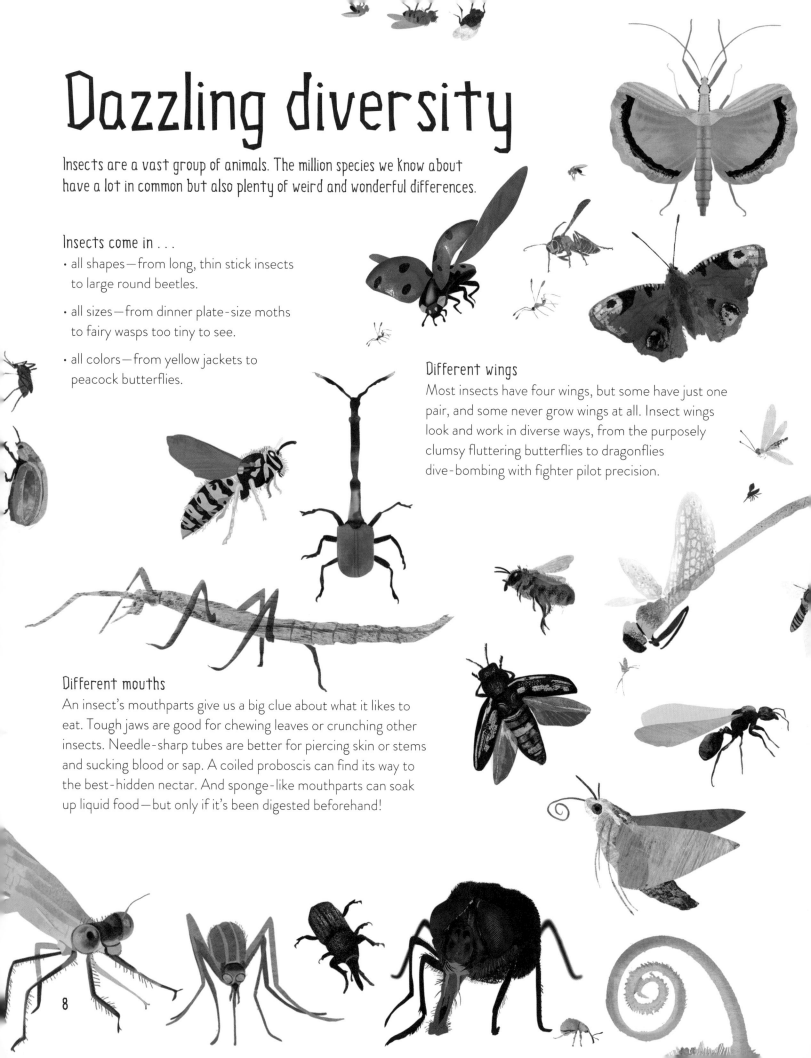

Different life cycles

Animals with a stiff exoskeleton can't grow gradually like we do. As they get bigger, they have to shrug off their cuticle like a coat that no longer fits and replace it with a larger one. This is called molting, and young insects do it all the time until they reach their adult form. All insects lay eggs, but there are three different routes to follow from egg to adult.

1. Some insects are born looking like tiny versions of their parents. These nymphs molt several times as they grow, until they are adults.

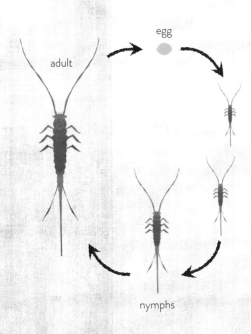

egg

adult

nymphs

2. Some insect nymphs look different from their parents. For example, they may have no wings, or they may live underwater instead of on land. With each molt, their body changes a little. This is called incomplete metamorphosis.

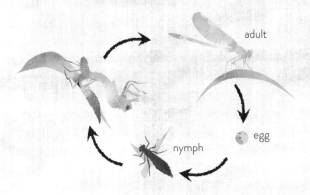

adult

egg

nymph

3. Most newly hatched insects look (and behave) completely differently from their parents. Their last molt is a very special one. They form a pupa and rest while their whole body is rearranged. This is how a caterpillar changes from a spongy blob to a beautiful butterfly.

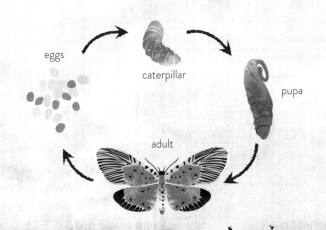

eggs

caterpillar

pupa

adult

Sorting insects

To help keep track of this dazzling diversity, scientists sort insects into smaller groups that share similar features. These groups are known as orders. Each chapter of this book explores one insect order, or group of closely-related orders. You'll meet some of the most common species (who still have plenty of secrets to share) and you'll also meet some rarer insects, with life cycles that boggle the mind (literally, if you happen to be a ladybug). Prepare to be delighted, disgusted, discombobulated, and dazzled.

True bugs

Did you know that "bug" isn't just another word for insect? Only around one in ten types of insects belong to the group known as "true bugs." At first glance, these insect families seem very different from one another. But look a little closer, and you'll find they have a lot in common.

Pale giant oak aphids

Sucking sap

True bugs feed by stabbing something (or someone!) with their needle- or beak-shaped mouthparts, then sucking out the juices inside. Most feed on plants, and large groups of aphids, scale insects, or whiteflies can damage crops.

Scale insects

These are the smallest true bugs. There are about 8,000 different types, but it's hard to get a good look at them. Most spend their lives underneath a hard shell or soft, waxy covering, making a plant look like it's covered in scales, such as these whiteflies.

Best breeders

There are thousands of species of aphids, and their superpower is producing more aphids! In a perfect aphid world (with no hungry predators and unlimited food), a single mother aphid could have BILLIONS of offspring. Each of these would go on to have billions more, and soon, Earth would be covered in a layer of aphids 93 miles (150 km) thick! Luckily, this doesn't happen because ladybugs, birds, and plenty of other creatures love to eat aphids.

Whiteflies feed underneath plant leaves. They are very unpopular with farmers and gardeners because they can spread viruses from plant to plant.

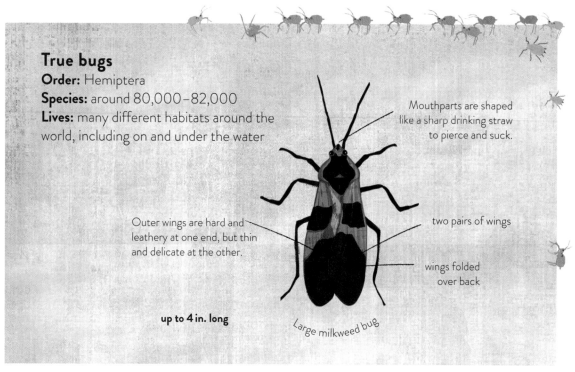

True bugs
Order: Hemiptera
Species: around 80,000–82,000
Lives: many different habitats around the world, including on and under the water

Mouthparts are shaped like a sharp drinking straw to pierce and suck.

two pairs of wings

Outer wings are hard and leathery at one end, but thin and delicate at the other.

wings folded over back

up to 4 in. long

Large milkweed bug

Ant farmers

Aphids and scale insects guzzle so much sugary sap that they poop out a sweet, sticky goo called honeydew. Ants think honeydew is completely delicious. Some types of ants live alongside aphids or scale bugs and act as tiny farmers, herding the bugs from place to place and protecting them from weather and predators. Their reward is unlimited honeydew.

Froghoppers and leafhoppers

Froghoppers are named for their froggy faces and amazing leaping skills. They're also known as spittlebugs because their nymphs like to hang out in bubbles of foamy froth. It's not really spit—the froghoppers make it by blowing air through slime. It hides them from predators and stops them from drying out on a warm day.

The peanut bug has eyespots and a lizard-like head to fool potential predators, but if that fails, it releases a smell like a skunk!

Bugs we eat

Have you ever eaten an insect? Unless you cook everything from scratch, the answer is almost certainly YES! Cochineal are tiny scale insects that live on cactus leaves. They can be dried and crushed up to make a bright red dye that is often used as food coloring. Many people don't like the idea of eating bugs, so on food labels it's listed as carmine, carminic acid, natural red 4, crimson lake, or E120.

Two-lined spittlebug

Cochineal scalel

11

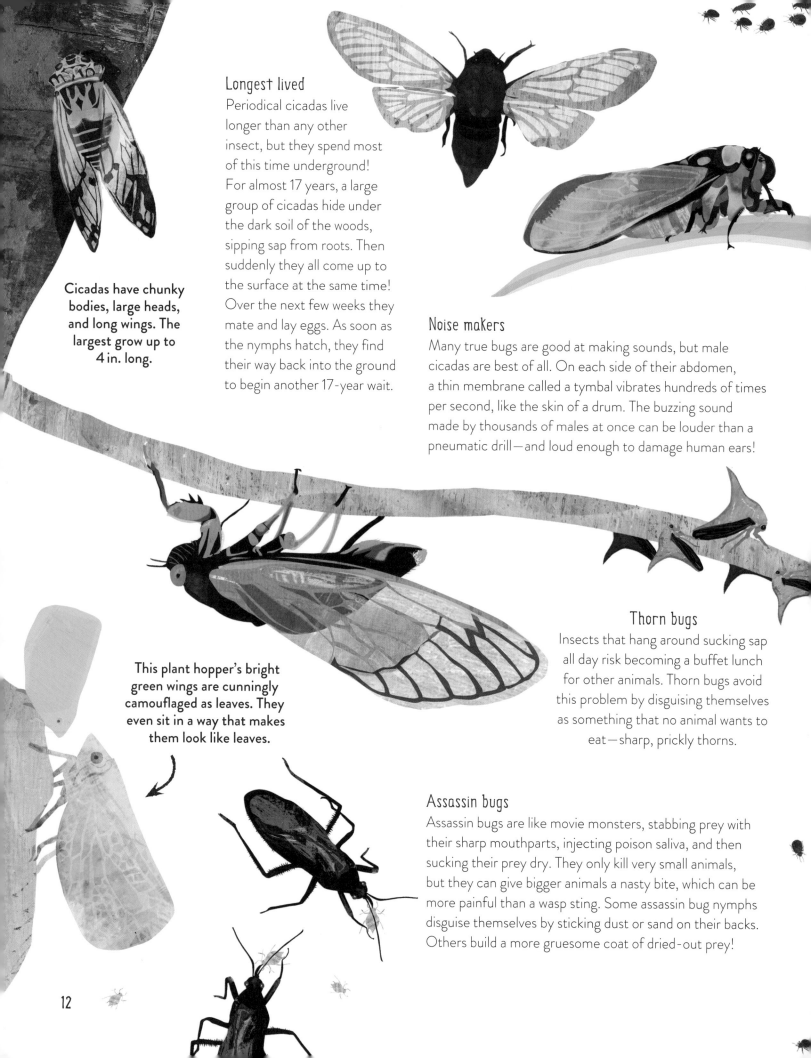

Longest lived

Periodical cicadas live longer than any other insect, but they spend most of this time underground! For almost 17 years, a large group of cicadas hide under the dark soil of the woods, sipping sap from roots. Then suddenly they all come up to the surface at the same time! Over the next few weeks they mate and lay eggs. As soon as the nymphs hatch, they find their way back into the ground to begin another 17-year wait.

Cicadas have chunky bodies, large heads, and long wings. The largest grow up to 4 in. long.

Noise makers

Many true bugs are good at making sounds, but male cicadas are best of all. On each side of their abdomen, a thin membrane called a tymbal vibrates hundreds of times per second, like the skin of a drum. The buzzing sound made by thousands of males at once can be louder than a pneumatic drill—and loud enough to damage human ears!

This plant hopper's bright green wings are cunningly camouflaged as leaves. They even sit in a way that makes them look like leaves.

Thorn bugs

Insects that hang around sucking sap all day risk becoming a buffet lunch for other animals. Thorn bugs avoid this problem by disguising themselves as something that no animal wants to eat—sharp, prickly thorns.

Assassin bugs

Assassin bugs are like movie monsters, stabbing prey with their sharp mouthparts, injecting poison saliva, and then sucking their prey dry. They only kill very small animals, but they can give bigger animals a nasty bite, which can be more painful than a wasp sting. Some assassin bug nymphs disguise themselves by sticking dust or sand on their backs. Others build a more gruesome coat of dried-out prey!

Water bugs

A host of different true bugs live in—or on—water. They include this giant water bug, which grows to about the size of your palm! These big beasts are fearsome predators and will even hunt small fish and frogs underwater.

Bed biters

Not all true bugs suck sap. Some use their mouthparts to pierce animal skin for a more meaty meal. Bed bugs have the worst reputation. By day they hide in nooks and crannies. By night they bite people and slurp their blood as they sleep. The bite itself doesn't hurt, but their saliva makes skin extremely itchy.

This water scorpion is named after its pincers, but its weirdest feature is on the other end of its body. Its "tail" is really a breathing tube, which works like a snorkel.

The backswimmer swims by lying on its boat-shaped back and rowing through the water with its largest pair of legs.

Stinky smells

Stink bugs are also called shield bugs because of their shape. But their real defense is the bad-smelling, bad-tasting chemicals they can squirt from their thorax.

Startling colors

Some stink bugs are the same color as the plants they eat, so they blend in. Others glimmer with bright, iridescent markings to warn other creatures that they taste bad!

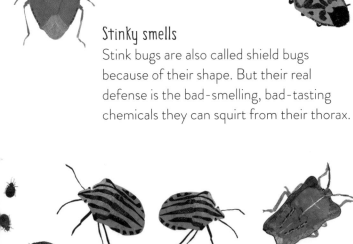

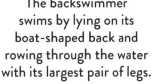

13

Lice and thrips

Let's meet some insects so tiny that we barely notice them—even when they're living in our homes or on our bodies! The biggest insects in these groups grow to just a few millimeters long. The smallest is so tiny you might mistake them for moving specks of dust.

A human habitat

Sucking and biting lice are parasites, which means they live their lives on a larger animal without giving anything back in return. How rude! A couple of types of sucking lice even live on humans, including head lice. Each female head louse lays around 10 eggs every day, gluing them to hair so they don't wash off. They are usually harmless, although their bites can be itchy.

Pollinators

Like other sap-sucking insects, thrips can damage plants when they bite through stems and steal the food the plant made for itself! But some thrips like to feed on nectar, flowers, and pollen. As they eat, they get completely covered in pollen and might even help pollinate plants like bees do.

Book lovers

Book lice live indoors. As their name suggests, they are sometimes spotted in old books, but they don't eat paper —just any mold and fungi growing on it. They're sometimes spotted in flour and other dried foods too, but they aren't strong enough to dig their way into packets, so they don't usually do any harm.

Book lice

Storm bugs

Bark lice

14

Elephant lice

Imagine trying to bite through an elephant's tough skin! It's all in a day's work for elephant lice, whose snouts have special biting mouthparts on the ends.

Storm bugs

Thrips often start flying around in the kind of weather that leads to thunderstorms, so in some places they're nicknamed thunder flies and storm bugs. Thrips that are attracted to brightly colored flowers tend to gather on brightly colored clothes too. A whole crowd of soccer fans once found themselves coated in thrips that had landed on their bright yellow shirts.

Grain thrips

The young ears of wheat and other grains are another good place to look for thrips. Tap the grains on a sheet of white paper and look carefully at any specks that fall out . . . especially those that get up and run away!

Grain thrips

Sucking and biting lice

Order: Phthiraptera
Species: around 3,150–5,000
Lives: on or near larger animals

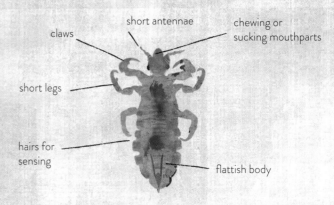

short antennae

chewing or sucking mouthparts

claws

short legs

hairs for sensing

flattish body

0.03 to 0.4 in. long

Thrips

Order: Thysanoptera
Species: around 5,000–6,000
Lives: mostly on plants

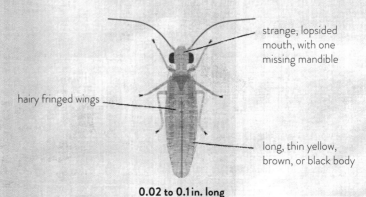

strange, lopsided mouth, with one missing mandible

hairy fringed wings

long, thin yellow, brown, or black body

0.02 to 0.1 in. long

Book lice and bark lice

Order: Psocoptera
Species: around 3,000–5,000
Lives: under bark and dead leaves; a few species live indoors

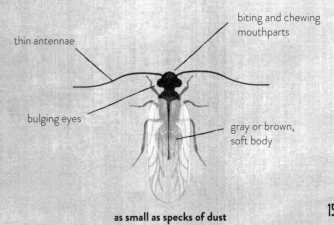

biting and chewing mouthparts

thin antennae

bulging eyes

gray or brown, soft body

as small as specks of dust

15

Earwigs, web spinners, and angel insects

Hidden away in dark places by day, these insects mainly move and feed at night. You may never spot one unless you lift a stone or disturb a pile of leaves. They can be fierce fighters, skilled weavers, and loving parents. They even help clear and recycle dead and rotting plants.

Recycling

Most earwigs feed at night, munching on dead plant material or hunting slow-moving creepy-crawlies such as aphids and scale insects! Earwigs help break down dead plants, so they are good creatures to have in a yard. Some species can become pests, nibbling on plant roots or even living on rodents or bats.

Giant earwigs can grow longer than your little finger!

Terrible tools

Earwigs use their cerci in all sorts of different ways. It's like having a Swiss Army knife on your bottom! They can catch, kill, and carry prey, or help an earwig unfold and refold its hidden wings.

Loving parents

Mother earwigs guard their eggs carefully, even washing them to get rid of any fungi. They also stick around to collect food for the young nymphs. However, once the nymphs of the maritime earwig molt for the second time, they make a hasty exit so they don't become a meal for their own mother!

Silk umbrellas

Web spinners live on tree bark and on forest floors, where they nibble dead plants and lichens. They weave huge silk nests over their heads. As they run back and forth along their silky tunnels, these tiny insects are safe from hungry predators such as ants. The silk also stops the web spinners and their eggs from getting washed away by heavy tropical rain!

Like earwigs, female web spinners are caring parents. Some even feed their nymphs with pre-chewed food!

Tiny angels

Angel insects are some of the world's smallest insects. Even the giants among them are just 0.2 inches long! They live together in groups of a few dozen (sometimes alongside termites) and eat fungi as well as roundworms and mites.

Earwigs
Order: Dermaptera
Species: around 2,000
Lives: in the soil, under stones, and in other dark places, especially in tropical, humid areas

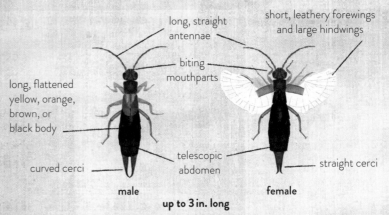

long, straight antennae

short, leathery forewings and large hindwings

biting mouthparts

long, flattened yellow, orange, brown, or black body

telescopic abdomen

curved cerci

straight cerci

male

female

up to 3 in. long

Web spinners
Order: Embioptera
Species: around 170–450
Lives: tropical forests

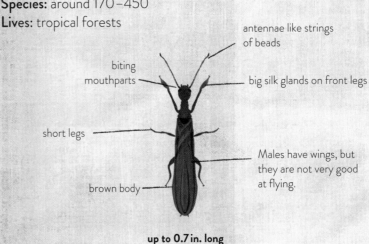

antennae like strings of beads

biting mouthparts

big silk glands on front legs

short legs

Males have wings, but they are not very good at flying.

brown body

up to 0.7 in. long

Angel insects
Order: Zoraptera
Species: around 30–35
Lives: mostly in tropical parts of world, in damp, rotting bark and logs

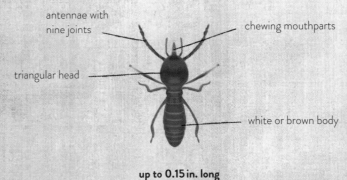

antennae with nine joints

chewing mouthparts

triangular head

white or brown body

up to 0.15 in. long

Stone flies, rock crawlers, and heelwalkers

The insects on this page have been around since before the time of the dinosaurs. Today they can be found hiding under rocks in some of the world's most extreme environments, only coming out at night.

Watery birth

Stone flies start their lives in the water. Females fly across the water, dropping eggs like tiny bombs or dipping their tails in the water so the eggs are washed off. When the nymphs hatch, they look a little bit like earwigs with two tails.

Stone fly nymphs molt up to 30 times before they become adults, which takes years! Much of this time is spent hiding under stones, venturing out to nibble algae and other water plants. When it's finally time to hatch into an adult, they crawl out of the water onto a rock or stone, molt for the last time, and spread their new wings.

Both stone flies and heelwalkers "talk" by tapping their bodies on the ground. Each species has its own pattern of drumming, like insect Morse code.

Human threats

These ancient insects have called Earth home for hundreds of millions of years but are now under threat from humans. Stone flies are easily harmed by polluted water, so it's rare to see one near a town or city. If you do spot a stone fly, it shows that the water is clean and fresh. Most rock crawlers can't survive if they get much warmer than 57°F, so heat waves caused by global warming are worrying.

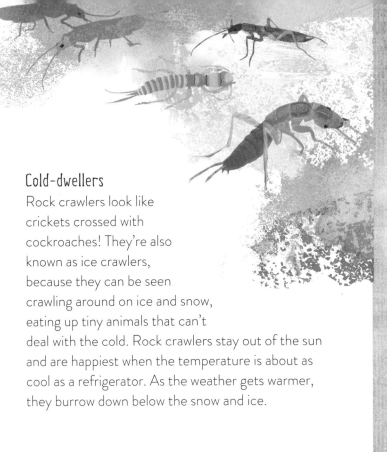

Cold-dwellers

Rock crawlers look like crickets crossed with cockroaches! They're also known as ice crawlers, because they can be seen crawling around on ice and snow, eating up tiny animals that can't deal with the cold. Rock crawlers stay out of the sun and are happiest when the temperature is about as cool as a refrigerator. As the weather gets warmer, they burrow down below the snow and ice.

Gladiators

Only a few species of heelwalkers have been found so far. They all seem to be predators, and some can capture prey the same size as themselves! These formidable fighting skills have earned them the nickname "gladiator bugs."

Stone flies
Order: Plecoptera
Species: 2,000–3,500
Lives: streams and rivers around the world

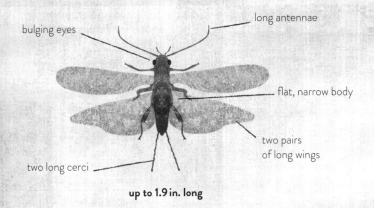

bulging eyes

long antennae

flat, narrow body

two pairs of long wings

two long cerci

up to 1.9 in. long

Rock crawlers
Order: Grylloblattodea
Species: around 30
Lives: cold mountains of North America and East Asia

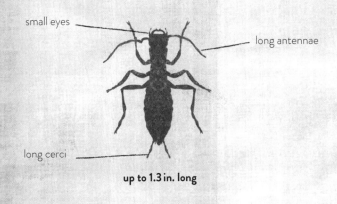

small eyes

long antennae

long cerci

up to 1.3 in. long

Heelwalkers
Order: Mantophasmatodea
Species: around 20
Lives: shrubs and grasses of sub-Saharan Africa

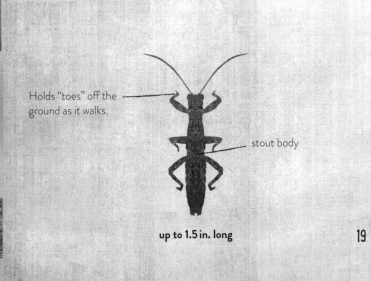

Holds "toes" off the ground as it walks.

stout body

up to 1.5 in. long

Grasshoppers, locusts, crickets, and katydids

You'll hear these insects before you see them! Grasshoppers and crickets fill the air with noisy chirping. They make these sounds to attract mates, but they can also attract predators. Luckily these long-legged athletes can use their powerful hind legs to leap away from danger.

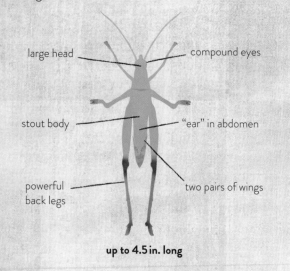

Grasshoppers and locusts
Sub order: Caelifera
Species: 12,000
Lives: grasslands and marshes around the world

large head

compound eyes

stout body

"ear" in abdomen

powerful back legs

two pairs of wings

up to 4.5 in. long

Vegetarians

Grasshoppers spend their days sitting in long grass, chewing away at its tough leaves. Many grasshoppers are green or brown to blend in with the plants. However, variegated grasshoppers have bright colors to warn predators that they are full of disgusting-tasting toxins from the plants they eat!

Insect musicians

Grasshoppers chirp by scraping their back legs against their wings. Each species makes a different sound so they can tell each other apart. To do this, grasshoppers have tiny versions of our eardrums on their bodies!

Swarm!

Locusts look like large grasshoppers but they can behave very differently. When their habitat starts to get crowded, locusts fly off in huge groups called swarms to search for more food. A big swarm includes up to 50 billion insects. Each locust can eat its own weight in food each day, which means a swarm can easily destroy entire fields of crops before flying off to find more.

Grasshoppers prefer to jump away from danger if they can, but if the large North American grasshopper is attacked, it raises its wings. If the flash of color doesn't scare predators away, it can release a stinky liquid that will!

Matchstick grasshoppers have long bodies and pointed heads, making them look like small twigs.

Matchstick grasshopper

Australia's sandgropers make sounds in a different way—by rubbing their mouthparts together!

Crewickets

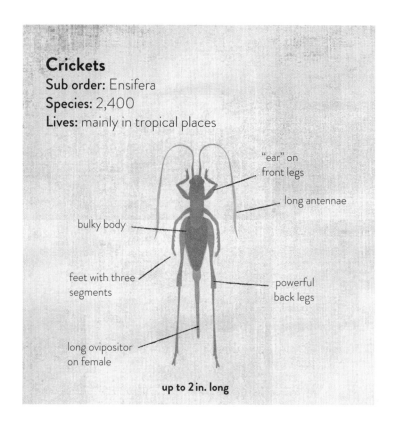

Crickets
Sub order: Ensifera
Species: 2,400
Lives: mainly in tropical places

"ear" on front legs

long antennae

bulky body

feet with three segments

powerful back legs

long ovipositor on female

up to 2 in. long

Meat eaters

Crickets and katydids aren't fans of grass—they like to eat other insects. They can even give a person a nasty bite. Crickets are bulkier than grasshoppers, not a fan of flying, and don't even like jumping that much! True katydids rely on disguise to keep them hidden as they climb around trees. Their green bodies and wide wings look just like leaves.

Field cricket

Noise makers

Crickets are even noisier than grasshoppers. They sing by rubbing their forewings together. Each wing has a line of tiny "teeth" like the ones you'd see on a saw, so the rubbing causes vibrations. Male crickets use different songs to attract mates and to tell other males to stay away.

Laying eggs

The back of a female cricket's or katydid's body is specially shaped to help them lay eggs in soil or inside the stems of plants. They dig a small burrow and then push their ovipositor into the hole to lay the eggs in a safe place.

Mole cricket

This strange-looking insect is in a different family from other crickets. Like a mole, it has huge front "claws" for digging underground burrows! It's even coated in velvety hairs to help it slide through the soil. It's hard to be heard when you're hiding underground, so mole crickets build a specially shaped chamber to boost the volume of their calls, which acts like a loudspeaker.

Mole cricket

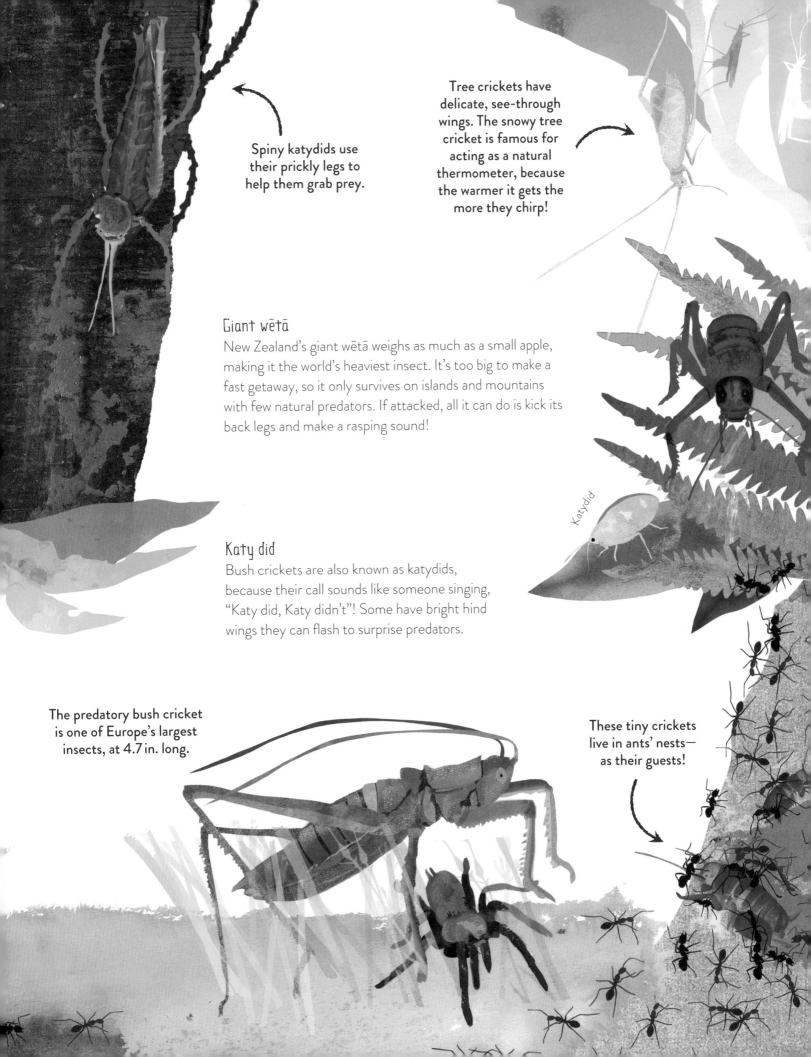

Spiny katydids use their prickly legs to help them grab prey.

Tree crickets have delicate, see-through wings. The snowy tree cricket is famous for acting as a natural thermometer, because the warmer it gets the more they chirp!

Giant wētā

New Zealand's giant wētā weighs as much as a small apple, making it the world's heaviest insect. It's too big to make a fast getaway, so it only survives on islands and mountains with few natural predators. If attacked, all it can do is kick its back legs and make a rasping sound!

Katydid

Katy did

Bush crickets are also known as katydids, because their call sounds like someone singing, "Katy did, Katy didn't"! Some have bright hind wings they can flash to surprise predators.

The predatory bush cricket is one of Europe's largest insects, at 4.7 in. long.

These tiny crickets live in ants' nests— as their guests!

Cockroaches, termites, and mantises

Mantises are some of the world's most beautiful insects. But beneath their beautiful looks, they are fearsome predators! Mantises are closely related to cockroaches and termites, but you'll find that these "pests" include some of the best architects, caring parents, and helpful recyclers in the animal kingdom.

Waste disposal

Cockroaches have a bad reputation for breaking into buildings, spoiling food, and spreading germs. In fact, just 40 types of cockroaches like living alongside humans. Thousands of other species prefer scavenging in clean, natural habitats such as forest floors. Wood roaches help get rid of nature's toughest waste—dead wood!

Madagascan hissing cockroach

German cockroach

Pssst!

Madagascan hissing cockroaches make this sound by pushing air out of breathing holes on their sides. The sound startles predators or warns other cockroaches away.

Colossus cockroach

Giant burrowing cockroach

Pill cockroach

Most cockroaches hide from light when they can—their Latin name even means "avoiding light"! But this strange cockroach makes its own light! The bioluminescence fools predators into thinking it's another glowing insect—a toxic click beetle.

Armored mothers

Pill cockroaches look like giant pill bugs! Underneath their tough armor, they are very caring parents. Mothers carry their nymphs under their bodies. They feed by sucking liquid out of special holes in her legs!

The world's largest cockroach weighs up to 1.8 oz. and lives underground, where it eats dead leaves.

Perfect predators

Praying mantises use their incredible camouflage and amazing vision to catch prey. When an unsuspecting insect or spider strolls or flies too close, the mantis pounces. Excellent eyesight and lightning-fast reactions means they rarely miss their target. Large mantises can catch frogs, lizards, and small birds. They can even grab flies in midair!

Cockroaches
Order: Blattodea
Species: 4,000–4,600
Lives: everywhere

long, thin antennae

shield-like head covering

large eyes

two pairs of wings

flat, oval body

spines on strong legs

up to 3.5 in. long

Mantises
Order: Mantodea
Species: more than 2,000–2,300
Lives: among plants in warm places

triangular head

Forward-facing eyes give mantises binocular vision.

very flexible neck

"ear" between front legs

spiny "claws"

long body and legs

up to 9.8 in. long

Ferocious flowers

Next time you see a beautiful flower, look very closely before you lean in and take a sniff. Flower mantises have bodies disguised to look like flowers. They even have parts that stick out like petals!

Some flower mantis nymphs look like ants.

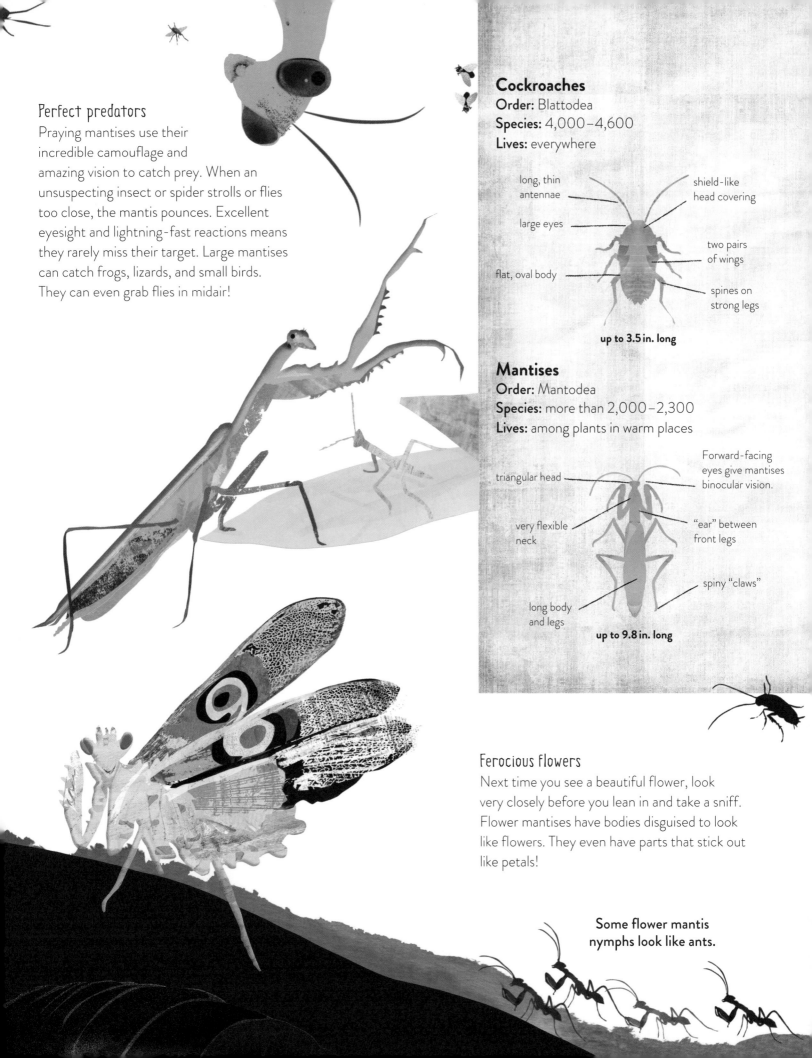

Animal architects

Some termites build incredible nests towering several yards above the ground. The termites begin by digging tunnels through soil or wood. The chewed-up wood or soil is mixed with termite spit or poop to make it more like cement. It's used to build structures full of tunnels, food supplies, gardens, and nurseries. Termites even build air vents to keep conditions inside exactly right and to stop their soft bodies from drying out. The biggest nests are cities with millions of termites! Not bad for blind insects the size of a grain of rice!

Magnetic termites sense Earth's magnetic field. They always line up their mounds north to south to make sure that no part of the nest gets too much of the hot Australian sun in one day.

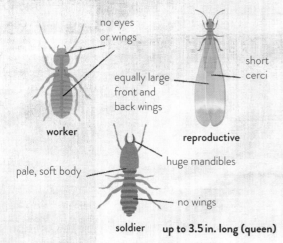

Termites

Order: Isoptera
Species: 2,500–3,000
Lives: tropical and subtropical parts of the world

no eyes or wings

equally large front and back wings

short cerci

worker

reproductive

pale, soft body

huge mandibles

no wings

soldier   **up to 3.5 in. long (queen)**

Drywood termite

Magnetic termite mound

Social roles

Inside these huge nests, different termites do very different jobs. The queen's job is to lay eggs—up to 40,000 in a day! Most of the nymphs that hatch become workers. Their job is to expand and take care of the nest and keep everyone clean and fed. A very few nymphs become reproductives, with wings so they can fly off and start their own nest.

The queen grows a hundred times larger than any other termite in the nest.

ventilation shaft

chimney

If you find yourself in a rain forest, look out for half a million termites marching in a line. Processional termites are the only ones to leave their nests in large groups, looking for food to carry back home.

nest

Globitermes termites

Fungus farmers

To help break down wood, termites need help from microbes. Some have friendly microbes living in their guts, but others grow gardens of fungus inside their nests! The workers bring dead wood back to the nest and let the fungus get to work. Then they feed the fungus to the colony.

Exploding soldiers

In some termite nests, certain nymphs become soldiers. Their job is to fight off enemies. Termite soldiers have special features that help them defend the nest, such as large heads and powerful mandibles. Some can spray sticky or toxic fluids to stop invading ants in their tracks. The most dramatic are these Southeast Asian termite soldiers, which explode their own bodies to cover enemies in a sticky goo.

Stick insects and leaf insects

Have you ever seen a twig with legs? Or looked at a leaf that looked back at you? Stick insects and leaf insects have some of the best camouflage. Most of these mimics move very s-l-o-w-l-y. Why run or fly when you can hide in plain sight?

Camouflage

By day these insects hide on plants, keeping as still as any other twig or leaf. If they have to walk, they sway to and fro, "juttering" like a stem quivering in the breeze. Birds, lizards, and other predators are fooled into thinking they are seeing part of a plant. Even if a predator comes too close, many stick insects keep in character. They fall to the ground and lie still like a dead twig!

Coconut stick insects startle predators (or rivals) by flashing their brightly colored wings.

Gray's leaf insect

Stick insects

Order: Phasmatodea / Phasmida
Species: around 3,000
Lives: warm climates, especially tropical forests

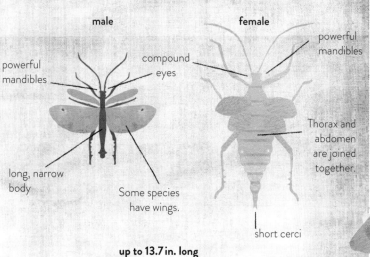

male

female

powerful mandibles

compound eyes

powerful mandibles

powerful mandibles

long, narrow body

Some species have wings.

Thorax and abdomen are joined together.

short cerci

up to 13.7 in. long

Walking leaves

Leaf insects and stick insects are closely related but very differently shaped. Leaf insects have broad, flattened bodies that look like leaves. Most are green, but some species look like dead, brown, or damaged leaves.

The largest leaf insects grow to just over 4 in.

Extra defenses

Even the best camouflage can't fool bats and other predators that hunt using sound instead of sight! Many stick insects have extra defenses. Some can shower enemies with stinky, toxic spray. The spray of the American walking stick irritates an animal's eyes so much that they are blinded for a while. Some stick insects lash out with spines on their legs. Others shed a leg instead!

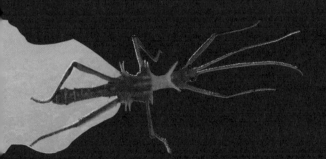

The touch-me-not stick insect has long spines. Would you dare to touch it?

Some female stick insects can reproduce without ever meeting a male stick insect. They simply lay eggs that develop into new females.

The long and short of it

The smallest stick insects could perch on your fingernail. Borneo is home to the longest stick insects ever found in the wild—the gargantuan females grow up to 22 inches (55 cm) long.

The return of the tree lobster

Lord Howe Island, Australia, was once home to thousands of giant stick insects known as "tree lobsters." In 1918, rats escaped onto the island from a wrecked ship and feasted on the local wildlife. For decades, the Lord Howe Island stick insects seemed to be extinct. But recently a few tree lobsters were rediscovered. They became famous as the world's rarest insects.

Darwin insect

Extraordinary eggs

Even stick insects' eggs are disguised! Many species lay eggs that look just like plant seeds. The eggs drop to the forest floor, where ants collect them and carry them into their nests as a snack. Hidden from predators and protected from forest fires, the stick insects gradually hatch. The nymphs of the spiny leaf insect even look like ants for extra protection!

Beetles

There are more types of beetles than any other animal on Earth. But all beetles have something in common: a pair of "shield wings" that act as a spectacular armor. There are beetles with rhino horns, giraffe necks, and elephant snouts. Beetles that are predators, parasites, and pollinators. There are even beetles that live, breed, and feast in piles of poop!

Cutting jaws

This stag beetle's long, spiny jaws are a tool for finding a mate. When two male stag beetles meet on the same branch, they use their jaws to grab their rival and throw him off the tree!

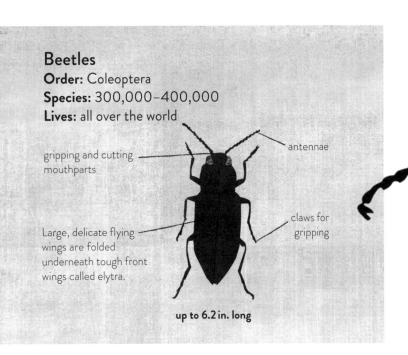

Beetles
Order: Coleoptera
Species: 300,000–400,000
Lives: all over the world

gripping and cutting mouthparts

antennae

claws for gripping

Large, delicate flying wings are folded underneath tough front wings called elytra.

up to 6.2 in. long

Goliath beetle

Shield wings

A beetle's tough "shield wings" are so unique the entire order is named after them! They make beetles tougher than most insects, allowing them to dig tunnels, have wrestling matches, go for a swim, or squeeze into cracks without damaging the flying wings hidden underneath. Most beetles must hold their wings out to the side as they fly, making them far less graceful than other insects!

Little and large

Beetles include some of the very smallest and very biggest insects. At less than 0.02 inches (0.5 mm) long, featherwing beetles are smaller than a pinhead. Goliath beetles are about the size of a mouse and weigh as much as an apple—making them some of the heaviest insects. Amazingly, they can still fly!

Cockchafer beetle

Colombian featherwing beetle

Trilobite beetles

The strangest-shaped beetles are the trilobite beetles of Southeast Asia. They are named after a type of extinct sea creature that had a similar flattened and segmented armored body. For years, scientists were confused because every trilobite beetle found was female! Males turned out to look much more like regular beetles—small, black, and winged.

Trilobite beetles

Very wet . . .

Some beetles are adapted to live watery lives. Their legs have bristly "paddles" for swimming. Watch out for whirligig beetles on the surface of ponds, lakes, and streams. They have two pairs of eyes—one for spotting underwater predators and one to look out for dead or injured insects on the surface. Yum!

Whirligig beetle

Great diving beetles can trap bubbles of air under their outer wings, allowing them to spend their time underwater hunting prey, such as tadpoles and small fish.

Brazil's titan beetles are the longest beetles, with jaws strong enough to snap a pencil in half.

. . . and very dry

Beetles living in dry deserts have the opposite problem. There are no ponds or lakes, and it rarely rains! This headstanding beetle uses its body to collect water from the air instead. Its bumpy outer wings attract water vapor in fog. Droplets of liquid water collect on the wings and run into channels that carry the water down toward the beetle's mouth.

A Madagascan giraffe weevil's super-long and flexible snout is used for wrestling other males.

Darkling beetles

Chemical defenses

If armor and weapons are not enough, some beetles have a third defense—spraying nasty chemicals from their bottoms! Bombardier beetles blast attackers with boiling liquid made by combining different chemicals in special chambers inside their bodies—sort of like a rocket!

Bombardier beetle

Some beetles are plain, dull, and masters of disguise. Others are among the brightest and most beautiful animals in the world. Meet the beetles that shimmer like rainbows, gleam like metal, and even glow in the dark!

Cardinal beetles

Jewel beetles

Although it seems like a jewel beetle's iridescent wings would make them easily spotted, they may help with camouflage! Iridescent objects appear to change color depending on the angle they are viewed from. This seems to confuse predators such as birds—and even humans!

Tamamushi beetles

Stay back!

Bright colors can be a warning signal. Oil beetles leak toxic liquid from their leg joints. It can give an animal bad blisters, so they're also known as "blister beetles." Predators learn to avoid their brightly patterned wings. Fire-colored beetles, who are mainly black, can't make their own poisons, so instead males climb onto blister beetles and lick the toxic chemicals off their wings! They pass the poison along to female fire-colored beetles, who use it to protect their eggs.

Frog-legged leaf beetle

Blister beetle

Rainbow leaf beetles

Leaf beetles

Leaf beetles can be just as beautiful as jewel beetles. The rainbow leaf beetle has stripes of metallic green, blue, gold, and red. The frog-legged leaf beetle has colorful shimmering legs and outer wings. Their legs are not used for leaping but for climbing and fighting!

Hide and seek

Harlequin beetles are named after their incredible patterns, which help camouflage them as they sip sap from trees covered in lichen and fungi. Like other longhorned beetles, they have very long antennae for sensing the world around them.

Harlequin beetle

Glowing beetles

If you spot a glowing insect, it's probably a beetle! Don't be fooled by their misleading names. Fireflies, or "lightning bugs," are actually beetles! The males flash their lights on and off as they fly to attract mates. Each of the 2,000 firefly species has its own pattern. The strange flashing may also ward off predators!

If click beetles find themselves on their backs, they can click their outer wings, pinging themselves into the air to land upright again. Some also have glowing spots on their heads or bodies. Even their eggs glow in the dark.

"Glowworms" are also beetles. Adult females have no wings. The tip of their abdomen glows with a greenish light to help flying males find them.

Whitest white

These scarab beetles are whiter than paper and whiter than snow. Their total lack of color is good camouflage against the white fungi they live on. Scientists are learning how to make paper, paints, and teeth whiter by studying them!

Click beetle

Cyphochilus beetle

Color changing

As the air gets wetter, this longhorn beetle changes from iridescent greenish-gold to red. The change happens as a special layer in their wing case soaks up water, swells up, and changes the way light is reflected from tiny scales.

Dress to impress

The larvae of some beetles, such as the green tortoise beetle, have bodies covered in spikes or spines. They are used to carry a "costume" made of dead skin and droppings.

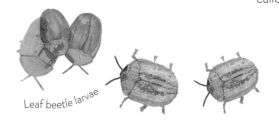
Australian tiger beetle

Tiger beetles

Ground beetles spend their lives on the ground, and most can't fly at all. Instead, they have long legs for running fast! This Australian tiger beetle can run at up to 5.5 miles per hour. Perhaps it should be called a cheetah beetle!

Leaf beetle larvae

So many beetles share our planet and shape our lives in different ways. Some species are loved by humans, and others are thought of as pests—depending on what they like to eat! But overall beetles are a vital part of life on Earth—as pollinators, predators, and recyclers.

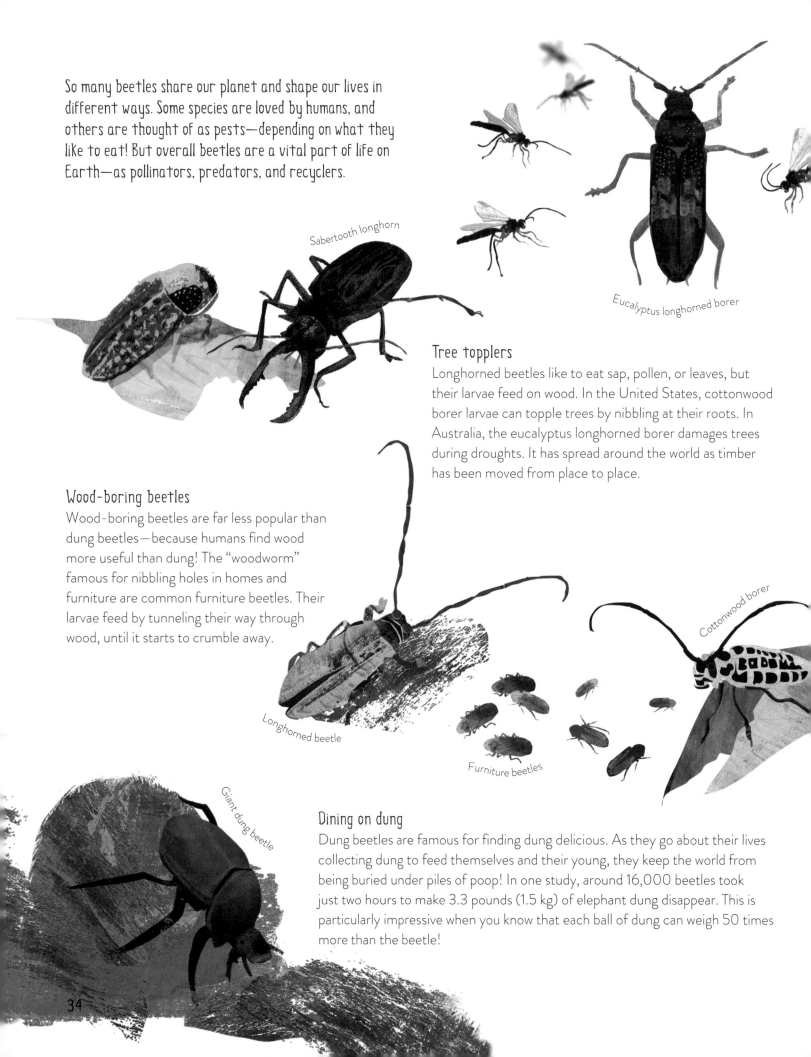

Sabertooth longhorn

Eucalyptus longhorned borer

Tree topplers

Longhorned beetles like to eat sap, pollen, or leaves, but their larvae feed on wood. In the United States, cottonwood borer larvae can topple trees by nibbling at their roots. In Australia, the eucalyptus longhorned borer damages trees during droughts. It has spread around the world as timber has been moved from place to place.

Wood-boring beetles

Wood-boring beetles are far less popular than dung beetles—because humans find wood more useful than dung! The "woodworm" famous for nibbling holes in homes and furniture are common furniture beetles. Their larvae feed by tunneling their way through wood, until it starts to crumble away.

Cottonwood borer

Longhorned beetle

Furniture beetles

Giant dung beetle

Dining on dung

Dung beetles are famous for finding dung delicious. As they go about their lives collecting dung to feed themselves and their young, they keep the world from being buried under piles of poop! In one study, around 16,000 beetles took just two hours to make 3.3 pounds (1.5 kg) of elephant dung disappear. This is particularly impressive when you know that each ball of dung can weigh 50 times more than the beetle!

A world of weevils

So far scientists have named more than 60,000 different species of weevils. New weevils are being discovered all the time. Most are adapted to be great at eating just one type of plant, which can cause big problems if that plant also happens to feed humans. Long snouts with jaws at the very tip help weevils to reach food other insects can't.

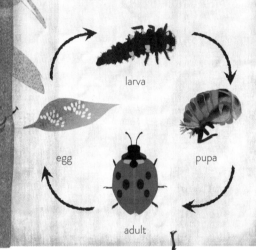

larva

egg

pupa

adult

Recycling heroes

Mealworm beetle larvae are usually thought of as pests because they like to chomp their way through grain. But they also seem to be able to eat and digest polystyrene (Styrofoam)! This plastic normally takes hundreds of years to break down naturally, so these beetles may become recycling heroes.

The Australian "stink beetle" eats caterpilllars that feed on crops.

Friend or foe?

Many beetles are predators, including ladybugs. They are popular with gardeners and farmers because their favorite food is plant-eating aphids (page 11). In the past, ladybugs have even been introduced to new parts of the world to control aphids. However, this can also cause problems. When Asian lady beetles run out of aphids to eat, they start eating native insects instead.

Pollinators

Long before bees, butterflies, and moths appeared on Earth, beetles were busy pollinating plants! As they visit flowers (usually to eat them), pollen sticks to their legs and bodies and gets carried from plant to plant. If a flower has a strong, overripe smell, it's a sign it may be pollinated by beetles! The most famous is the gigantic titan arum flower, which smells like rotting meat.

Seven-spotted ladybugs

Flies

Flies are the insects most often seen (and heard) in our homes—but also some of the least welcome! Some flies' fondness for dead animals and dung have earned them a bad reputation for spreading diseases. You might be used to swatting flies away from your food, but if you get to know your nearest insect neighbors better, you'll find out just how important they are.

True flies
Order: Diptera
Species: up to 150,000
Lives: every continent except Antarctica

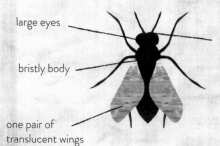

large eyes

bristly body

Mouthparts suck up or soak up food; some can pierce or cut too.

one pair of translucent wings

up to 2.7 in. long

The more lenses in a compound eye, the better the insect can see. But this takes up space —a big-headed fly's eyes cover its entire head!

Feet produce tiny drops of sticky fluid. Flies can climb and sit on any surface, even upside down.

This giant robber fly grows up to 2 in. long—as long as your little finger!

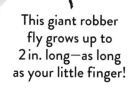

Robber flies
Robber flies look dangerous, with bristly hairs and a sharp proboscis ready to stab prey. But don't worry—they never try to eat humans! Robber flies prey on insects, from beetles and butterflies to grasshoppers and dragonflies. Some even pounce on bees in midflight! After injecting their prey with digestive juices, they suck up the insect soup.

Medical marvels

Fly eggs hatch into larvae (called maggots), which then develop into adult flies—all within three weeks! Maggots are pale and have no legs, so they wriggle around eating as much as they can. They are important decomposers, breaking down dead animals and dung. Greenbottle maggots are sometimes used to clean infected wounds in hospitals, where they work faster than medicines or dressings and can destroy even the nastiest bacteria!

Mosquitoes

This huge family of flies have long, slender legs, and mouthparts that female mosquitoes use to pierce the skin of animals and suck their blood. These parasites can spread certain diseases that are carried in blood. In some parts of the world, this includes serious diseases, such as malaria and yellow fever.

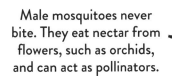

Male mosquitoes never bite. They eat nectar from flowers, such as orchids, and can act as pollinators.

Black flies are also known as buffalo gnats and sandflies in some parts of the world.

A female horsefly's eyes are wide apart, while a male's touch in the middle or even join smoothly together. It's worth learning to tell them apart, because only the females bite!

Horseflies

Horseflies don't pierce skin and suck blood out like mosquitoes. Instead, their mouthparts slice an animal's skin, causing a small pool of blood to well up to the surface. Horseflies can drink as much as a mug full of blood from a single cow in one day. For humans, a horsefly bite can be extremely painful.

Blowflies

Big, hairy blowflies are nicknamed bluebottles and greenbottles for their metallic shine. Unlike most of the animal kingdom, they are big fan of dung and dead animals—this is where they like to eat and to lay their eggs. In the winter months they like to find shelter and warmth in our homes, where they lay their eggs on food instead.

The flies you've just met are Known for feasting on disgusting dinners, but not all flies are insect-eating predators or bloodsucking parasites. Most flies eat plants or decaying matter and play important roles in Earth's ecosystems. Without them, we'd be Knee deep in rotting fruit and dung!

Midges and gnats

Clouds of tiny flies can often be seen dancing in the air at dusk and dawn. Many species don't bite, but those that do can cause MAJOR itching as they steal a sip of our blood. However, even biting midges have important roles to play. Males sip nectar rather than blood and are important pollinators of plants, including cacao trees—the source of chocolate!

Gall midge

These small midges trick plants into growing tiny shelters around their maggots! The growths are known as galls. They can damage plants, but many species make up for this by nibbling other plant pests, such as aphids and mites.

Hoverflies

You might mistake a hoverfly for a yellow jacket or bee at first glance—an adaptation that helps keep predators away. But they prefer plants to picnics. Their larvae have less dainty eating habits, chowing on soft insects, rotting vegetables, or dung!

Bee flies

These plump, hairy flies mimic bumblebees. This helps them get close enough to bee nests to lay their eggs. It also deters predators, so the flies can safely hover in front of flowers, sucking nectar. It's a clever trick, as bee flies can't really sting. Another way to tell the difference is to listen carefully—a bee fly's wings whine rather than buzz.

Glow-in-the-dark maggots

Look inside certain caves in New Zealand and underneath certain logs in Brazil, and you'll see glowing pinpricks of blue light—made by glowing fungus gnat maggots!

Fruit flies

Fruit flies are tiny and delicate, with bright eyes and pretty, patterned wings. These flies seek out fruit to lay their eggs in. The pointed part at the end of a fruit fly's body is not a tail, but an "ovipositor" to help females get their eggs deep down into the fruit. This means they can damage crops— but certain fruit flies are used by farmers as a natural weapon against weeds!

Fruit flies beat their tiny wings more than 200 times per second!

Vinegar flies

Vinegar flies

These fruit flies are also known as vinegar flies because of their love of rotting fruit. They are important decomposers, breaking down fruit that doesn't get eaten. They have also played a starring role in science, thanks to amazing similarities between human and vinegar fly genes!

Crane flies

Leggy crane flies are easy to recognize—especially because they love to visit lit-up homes at night. Their long legs, wings, bodies, and heads make them seem large, but they are harmless—most live in grass and don't have mouthparts to feed at all, let alone bite!

Stalk-eyed signal flies

Stalk-eyed signal flies live in tropical areas of Australasia. They have eyes on long stalks that stick out from the sides of their heads like antlers. Males even use them to battle other males for territory! However, most battles are won without fighting—the males with shorter eyestalks will back off and leave the area.

Adult crane flies' delicate, long legs are adapted to break off easily if caught, so they can get away.

Fleas, stylops, and scorpion flies

Fleas and stylops are parasites, living on (or inside) live animals and stealing a snack when they can! Scorpion flies have a less lethal but even more disgusting diet. They can be spotted chewing on dead insects, mold, and even bird droppings. If you haven't lost your appetite yet, you're about to . . .

Bloodsuckers

Fleas are only interested in one meal—fresh blood! Perfectly adapted parasites, their small bodies slip easily between hairs and feathers with no wings to get in the way. But if an animal tries to brush or scratch them off, their bristly bodies ensure they stay stuck where they are.

Hop on, hop off

Adult fleas only need to hop on to their host when they want to suck blood. Most of the time the fleas—and their eggs and larvae—are found in their host's bed, nest, or burrow. The larvae don't drink blood but gobble up the host's dead skin and other debris they find.

Human hosts

Most fleas aren't very picky about who they bite and will happily feed on human blood. They can spread disease-causing microbes from animals to humans—including the bacteria responsible for the bubonic plague. Fleas (and their rat hosts) caused the Black Death that killed a quarter of all Europeans in the Middle Ages.

Natural catapults

Fleas can't fly, so they rely on jumping to get from place to place. An elastic protein called resilin helps a flea catapult itself more than 100 times its own body length!

Lurking larvae

Bees, watch out. Inside flowers lurk parasites so disgusting they make fleas look friendly. Baby stylops position themselves in places that larger insects such as bees like to visit. They hitch a ride back the nest, where they invade the bee larvae. Rather than killing the larva, they live inside it as it grows up and becomes an adult bee!

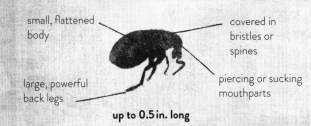

Life in a bee's bottom

Male stylops eventually crawl out of the bee and fly away, but females will live inside their host for the rest of their life. Female stylops have no legs or wings. Most of their body stays hidden in their host, but their head pokes out! They release smelly chemicals that tell male stylops where they are.

Odd insects

Scorpion flies are neither scorpions nor flies! Scientists still aren't sure where they fit on the insect family tree, but some seem to be closely related to fleas. The male scorpion fly's scary-looking tail is not really a stinger, but parts adapted for mating.

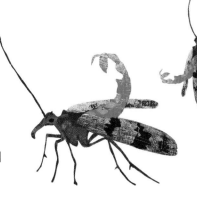

Snow fleas

These scorpion flies are known as "snow fleas." Like fleas, they can't fly, so they catapult themselves around instead. They can be spotted on moss and on snow, hoovering up microbes such as mold.

Fleas
Order: Siphonaptera
Species: 2,600
Lives: all around the world, on or near mammals or birds

small, flattened body

covered in bristles or spines

large, powerful back legs

piercing or sucking mouthparts

up to 0.5 in. long

Stylops
Order: Strepsiptera
Species: around 600
Lives: around the world

Halteres help with balance as they fly.

one pair of working wings

wingspan up to 0.2 in.

Scorpion flies
Order: Mecoptera
Species: around 550
Lives: gardens, hedgerows, and among damp leaf litter in woods

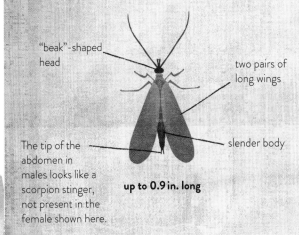

"beak"-shaped head

two pairs of long wings

slender body

The tip of the abdomen in males looks like a scorpion stinger, not present in the female shown here.

up to 0.9 in. long

Butterflies and moths

Everyone is familiar with butterflies and moths ... or are they? Did you know that there are nine times more moth than butterfly species? Or that the world's silk is produced by the hardworking caterpillars of a type of moth?

Scales

Each of a butterfly's overlapping scales has its own color. Together they form a picture—rather like pixels on a screen. The bright colors and patterns do different jobs. Some species, like this peacock butterfly, have wings that startle predators. The patterns may also help butterflies of the same species to recognize each other.

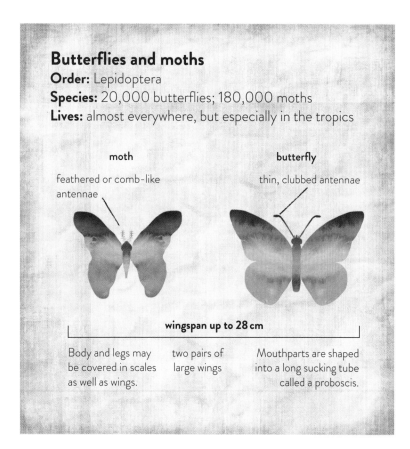

Butterflies and moths
Order: Lepidoptera
Species: 20,000 butterflies; 180,000 moths
Lives: almost everywhere, but especially in the tropics

moth	butterfly
feathered or comb-like antennae	thin, clubbed antennae

wingspan up to 28 cm

Body and legs may be covered in scales as well as wings.

two pairs of large wings

Mouthparts are shaped into a long sucking tube called a proboscis.

Parts of a glasswing butterfly's wing are see-through because they don't have scales.

Fluttering wings

Most adult butterflies only eat nectar from flowers. In order to visit enough flowers, they spend most of their time in the air. Their fluttering wings look clumsy, but this makes it hard for predators to predict which way the butterfly will fly! Bright colors are easy to spot by day, so butterflies rest with their wings closed together over their body. (In some species they are held together by interlocking hairs, like Velcro!)

The undersides of butterfly wings are duller for camouflage.

Painted ladies

Monarch butterflies

Mega migration

Some butterflies lead surprisingly long-haul lives. Painted lady butterflies can travel around 1,850 miles (3,000 km) from the parts of North Africa where they hatch to the Arctic Circle. Monarch butterflies migrate even farther, traveling from Mexico to Canada in huge swarms. However, no single butterfly makes the whole trip. It's more like a relay! After flying a few hundred miles, a butterfly stops to lay eggs. The next generation of butterflies then continues the journey.

Queen Alexandra's butterfly is the biggest species.

Cunning caterpillars

Most butterflies lay their eggs on plants so that the caterpillars hatch right on top of their favorite food. The only problem is avoiding becoming dinner themselves! Some caterpillars are covered with hairs or spines, or have bright warning colors to repel predators. Swallowtail butterfly caterpillars have a different trick. They avoid being eaten by looking like bird droppings, or simply by making a bad smell!

Swallowtail

Changing room

After eating their fill, butterfly caterpillars form a pupa called a chrysalis. This is often very well camouflaged. Inside, their bodies are totally rearranged into the form of the adult butterfly. This make take a few days . . . or several years.

Magical moths

Many moths are nocturnal, flying and feeding by night. This explains why many have dull wings, with patterns that blend in with the bark where they rest by day. But moths can be beautifully bright too.

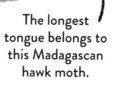

Oleander hawk moth

Coiled like a spring

Moths and butterflies can't chew pollen or leaves. Their upper jaws have practically disappeared, while their lower jaws have adapted into a long, thin tube made of the same springy protein that fleas use to jump. At rest, the tube is coiled up tightly, held together by tiny hairs like a natural zip. When the moth wants to eat, the proboscis unzips and becomes a drinking straw. After the meal, the moth relaxes its muscles and the tongue springs back into a coil.

The longest tongue belongs to this Madagascan hawk moth.

Male emperor moth

Amazing antennae

A male moth's huge, feathered antennae give him a super sense of smell. This male emperor moth can smell a female moth up to seven miles away—then fly in the right direction to find her!

Super sounds

Moths and butterflies aren't as silent as they seem. There are butterflies that hiss to scare enemies, and others that click as they fly. Some moths even make the same high-pitched noises made by bats. This may distract the bats (which love to feast on moths)—kind of like scrambling their radar!

Common garden micro moth

White witch moth

Gentle giants

Most moths that we see in and around our homes are micro moths, no bigger than a grain of rice. The smallest have wings that measure just 0.08 inches from tip to tip. But in tropical forests, you'll find moths that are as big as birds—and just as brightly colored.

The luna moth lives for just a week and doesn't eat at all. It doesn't even have a mouth! The food it ate as a caterpillar gives it enough energy to find a mate.

This owlet moth has an extrastrong proboscis which allows it to scratch skin and sip blood.

Very hungry caterpillars

Many people like to glimpse adult butterflies and moths, but their caterpillars aren't always as welcome. Some caterpillars damage the crops they nibble on or eat their way through things that human store, from grain to clothes. Hungriest of all are polyphemus moth caterpillars, which can eat 86,000 times their birth weight in tree leaves.

Hairy barbs

Some moth caterpillars are so hairy they are known as woolly bears. But they're not as pettable as they seem. Like the hairs of tarantulas, they have sharp barbs that work their way into skin, causing pain and itching.

Silk spinners

Moth caterpillars build a silk cocoon to protect themselves as they metamorphose into their adult form. Some use their silk for other reasons, too. For example, tent caterpillars build silky tents on trees to hide in between meals! Humans collect and use the silk made by silk moth caterpillars to make clothes and other items.

Caddis flies, alderflies, lacewings, and snake flies

You might mistake these insects for each other as they fly by on delicate wings crisscrossed with veins. They are close relatives but live very different lives in and around water. The lives of their larvae are stranger still. They can be found spinning silk, weaving nets, and building armor!

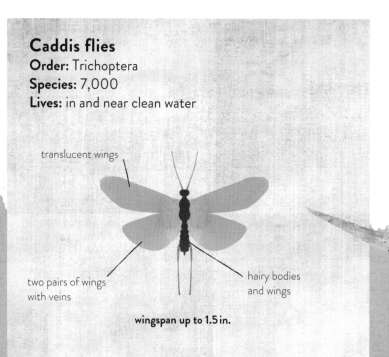

Caddis flies
Order: Trichoptera
Species: 7,000
Lives: in and near clean water

translucent wings

two pairs of wings with veins

hairy bodies and wings

wingspan up to 1.5 in.

Armor builders

Caddis fly larvae are some of the best insect engineers. To protect themselves from hungry fish, many species build their own tube-shaped armor from bits of sand, grit, grass, or anything else they find in the water. It's all glued together with strong silk.

When it's time for the larvae to molt for the last time, their armor forms a ready-made cocoon!

Wasp attack

This strategy isn't totally foolproof. There are two species of parasitic wasps that look for these tubes and lay their eggs inside. When the young wasp larvae hatch, they have a ready-made meal.

Snowflake caddis

Large caddis fly

Moth relatives

Adult caddis flies are most active as darkness falls. They are attracted to light, so they often get mistaken for moths. They are closely related to butterflies and moths, sharing the same scorpion fly ancestors.

Net weavers

Caddis fly larvae don't just use their engineering skills for protection. Some spin nets of silk in streams to fish for fragments of dead leaf . . . or dead insect. Their silk binds together river rocks, helping provide stable homes for all kinds of other creatures, too.

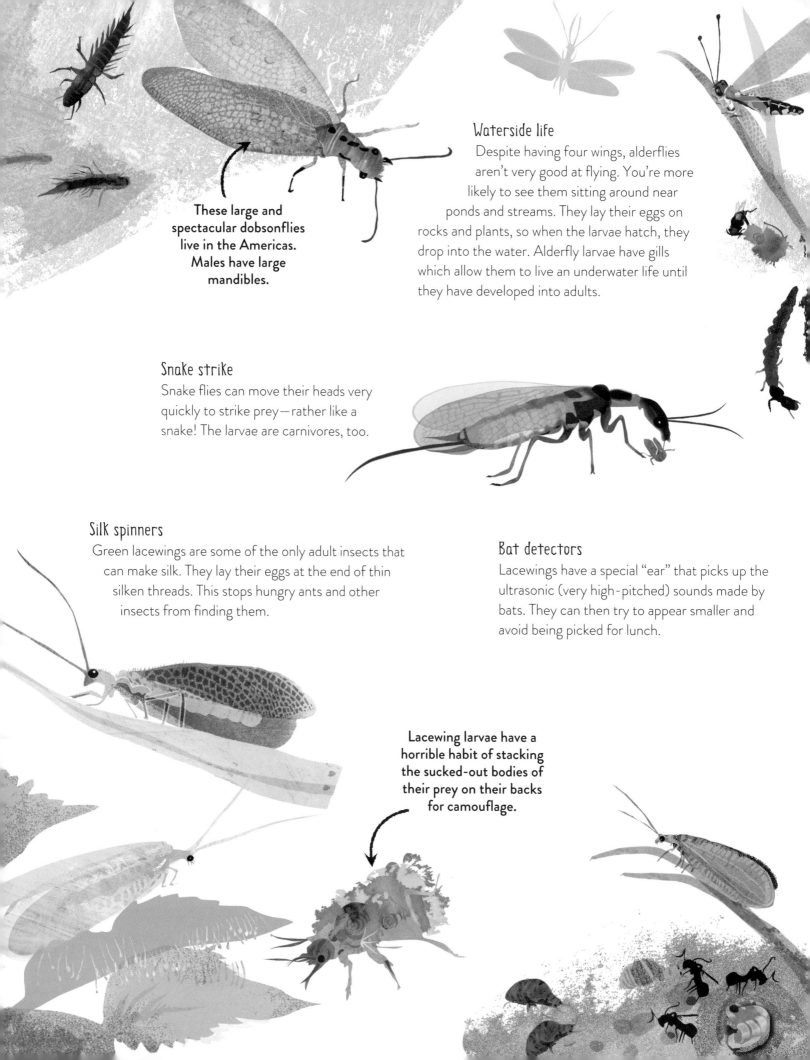

These large and spectacular dobsonflies live in the Americas. Males have large mandibles.

Waterside life

Despite having four wings, alderflies aren't very good at flying. You're more likely to see them sitting around near ponds and streams. They lay their eggs on rocks and plants, so when the larvae hatch, they drop into the water. Alderfly larvae have gills which allow them to live an underwater life until they have developed into adults.

Snake strike

Snake flies can move their heads very quickly to strike prey—rather like a snake! The larvae are carnivores, too.

Silk spinners

Green lacewings are some of the only adult insects that can make silk. They lay their eggs at the end of thin silken threads. This stops hungry ants and other insects from finding them.

Bat detectors

Lacewings have a special "ear" that picks up the ultrasonic (very high-pitched) sounds made by bats. They can then try to appear smaller and avoid being picked for lunch.

Lacewing larvae have a horrible habit of stacking the sucked-out bodies of their prey on their backs for camouflage.

Stand out, blend in

Owl-flies tend to be large and bright with extralarge haltheres. But owl-fly larvae look nothing like their parents. They are predators that sneak up on their prey by blending perfectly into the background . . .

Mantid flies

Is it a wasp? Is it a lacewing? Or is it a praying mantis? Mantid flies look like a mash-up of different insects and must be seen to be believed!

Ant lions

Ant lion larvae can be found hanging out at the bottom of tiny sandboxes, flinging sand at passing ants. If an ant falls in, it will be sucked dry and flung out again!

Alderflies, dobsonflies, and fish flies

Order: Megaloptera
Species: 300
Lives: near cool, clean water around the world

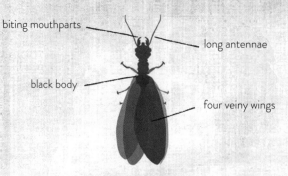

biting mouthparts

long antennae

black body

four veiny wings

wingspan up to 8.2 in.

Lacewings, mantid flies, owl-flies, and ant lions

Order: Neuroptera
Species: 5,000
Lives: in forests, backyards, and other habitats

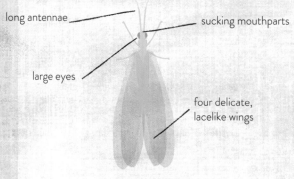

long antennae

sucking mouthparts

large eyes

four delicate, lacelike wings

wingspan up to 5.9 in.

Snake flies

Order: Raphidioptera
Species: 225
Lives: in trees

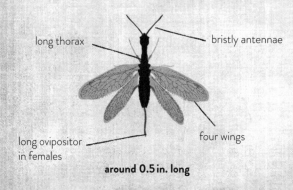

long thorax

bristly antennae

long ovipositor in females

four wings

around 0.5 in. long

Wasps, bees, and ants

We all think we know wasps, bees, and ants because they keep inviting themselves to our picnics. But this enormous group includes hundreds of thousands of members you haven't yet met, including important pollinators, annoying pests, and parasites with mind-blowingly complex life cycles.

Winged warriors

Wasps are famous for two things: building enormous nests and stinging anyone who gets too close to them. But only a few of the 30,000 different types of wasps share these habits. Most wasps live alone (or side by side in small groups) and don't sting.

Hunting wasps

Solitary hunting wasps use their stingers to catch prey. These potter wasps make a wasp-line for caterpillars. The venomous stinger paralyzes the caterpillar, making it easy to drag to where the wasp wants it—into a tiny "pot" that the wasp has made from mud. In each pot the wasp lays one egg. The motionless prey will provide fresh meat for the growing grubs.

Spider wasps

Parasitoid wasps go one step further, laying their eggs on or inside their prey. When the larvae hatch, they chomp their way through the living animal from the inside out! The adults prefer sweeter meals, such as nectar. This tarantula hawk wasp is as long as an adult's little finger, with wings more than four inches across. Its huge size allows it to attack tarantulas!

Ants, bees, and wasps
Order: Hymenoptera
Species: 280,000
Lives: almost everywhere

up to 2.3 in. long

two pairs of wings | chewing mouthparts | head that moves around easily | narrow "waist"

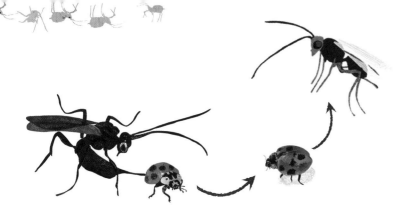

Zombie ladybugs

If you ever spot a ladybug behaving strangely, it may be a victim of this parasite wasp. The larvae nibbles on the insides of the ladybug, before forming a pupa beneath the beetle's body! At the same time as it lays the egg, the adult passes on a virus that infects the ladybug's brain. The effect of this is to make the ladybug stay very still—only twitching when a predator gets too close.

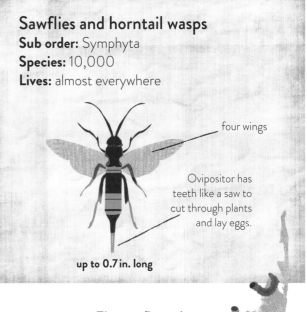

Sawflies and horntail wasps
Sub order: Symphyta
Species: 10,000
Lives: almost everywhere

four wings

Ovipositor has teeth like a saw to cut through plants and lay eggs.

up to 0.7 in. long

Elm sawfly grubs munch through leaves leaving zigzag patterns.

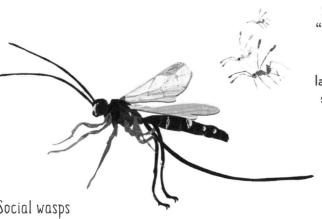

Saber wasps have long "tails" that are tubes for drilling into wood and laying eggs inside the larvae of other parasites, such as horntail wasps.

Social wasps

If you spot a huge, papery nest, stay clear—these belong to social wasps, who live in huge colonies. Workers build a home for the queen by chewing up plants and mashing the fibers together—like an enormous papier-mâché project! Inside the nests are hundreds of little rooms or "cells" where growing larvae can develop.

Humongous hornets

Hornets are the biggest wasps. Largest of all is the Japanese giant hornet, which lives all over Asia. Even its stinger is more than 0.2 inches long. It delivers a nasty poison that kills dozens of people every year. However, hornets are less likely to sting than their smaller cousins. They prey on honeybees, raiding their nests and chopping off their heads using their fearsome mandibles.

Paper wasps can tell each other apart by their facial markings.

Busy bees

There are TONS of reasons to love bees. They only sting in self-defense—unlike wasps, honeybees usually die after stinging. Most only eat nectar and pollen, even turning it into delicious honey. And all bees support life on Earth by pollinating flowering plants—including most of the crops that we eat!

Foraging from flowers

There are more than 20,000 types of bees, but they all live in places where there are flowers to find. Bees fly from flower to flower, sucking up nectar through their long proboscises and often gathering pollen to take back to their nest.

Giant carpenter bee

Solitary bees

Some bees live alone, or in small groups, side by side. Each female builds her own nest, lays her own eggs, and collects food for her own larvae to eat. Male solitary bees don't have nests. They can be spotted dozing on plant stems or even napping inside flowers!

Wallace's giant bees are the biggest bees of all. They build their nests inside termite colonies. To keep the termites away, they line the walls with sticky tree resin.

Leaf-cutting bees

These North American bees are busy cutting shapes from leaves and using them like flat-pack furniture! Back at their nest, the rolled leaf is simply pushed into a hole and—presto!—a ready-made cell to lay their eggs in.

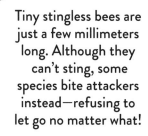

Tiny stingless bees are just a few millimeters long. Although they can't sting, some species bite attackers instead—refusing to let go no matter what!

Social bees

Some bees turn the nectar and pollen they collect into honey, which will last all year. Honeybees live in groups of up to 50,000, finding a hollow space to build a huge nest. The honeybees build their honeycombs from wax made by special glands in their abdomen. Humans harvest this beeswax for use in cosmetics and candles.

If a worker bee discovers a feast of flowers, they return back to the hive to perform a "waggle dance." This tells other bees which direction to fly and how far they need to go.

Colony

A honeybee colony is a giant family in which every bee has a certain job.

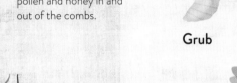

The youngest workers keep the nest clean and feed the growing grubs.

As they get older, workers begin making wax and become builders, or shift pollen and honey in and out of the combs.

Worker

Queen

The queen stays in the nest and lays eggs. Lots of eggs! She is taken care of by her daughters, the worker bees.

Grub

After a turn at guarding the nest, workers finally get to fly away and look for food themselves.

Bumblebees

Bumblebees also live in groups with a single queen, but their colonies are smaller. They take over abandoned animal dens or birdhouses, or snuggle inside compost heaps. Inside their nest, they work hard to keep the eggs warm. Some bumblebees have a special bald spot on their body to help their body heat pass to the eggs.

Furry helicopters

Bumblebee wings work more like helicopter rotors than flapping wings. The beating wings move so fast that they make a buzzing sound. The larger the bee, the lower the buzz. Listen carefully and you might hear a bumblebee do an extra special buzz each time it lands on a flower. This vibration helps shake pollen onto its body!

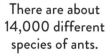

Amazing ants

Ants are close relatives of bees and wasps but rarely fly. They are very good at living life with their feet on the ground. In fact, scientists suspect that ants outnumber any other creature on Earth. Up to 10 quadrillion are crawling around the planet right now! Wherever ants live, they support ecosystems—letting air and water into soil and breaking down nature's waste so it can be recycled into new life.

There are about **14,000 different species of ants.**

Multitasking mandibles

An ant's mouthparts include a pair of mandibles for chewing up food. They also come in handy for cutting, digging, carrying, tending to grubs, catching prey, and driving predators away!

Unstoppable armies

Army ants of South America and driver ants of Africa are famous for marching in their millions, in parades up to 330 feet long. The marching ants eat anything in their path that can't run away.

Once bulldog ants lock their mandibles into prey, they don't let go easily. As if the bite weren't bad enough, they curl their abdomen in to deliver a painful sting too.

These "giant terrible" ants lock mandibles as they wrestle to defend their territory.

Central heating

Ants build their nests above and below the ground. Wood ants do it by piling pine needles around a rotting tree stump. As the wood decays, it heats the nest and keeps it cozy.

Living glue guns

Sometimes even grubs have jobs to do. Weaver ants build nests by folding leaves that are still attached to trees. It's no easy job for a tiny insect, so they work together—forming a chain of ants from one edge of a leaf to the other, then dropping out one by one until the edges touch. To stick them together, a larva is gently squeezed until it produces sticky silk—like a living glue gun!

All in the family

Like social wasps and bees, most of the ants you see are female. Colonies include a queen who lays eggs and thousands of female workers who can't lay eggs. Some also include soldier ants, with bodies adapted for defense. There are also a few males, who live long enough to fertilize eggs.

Worker ants collect food for the whole colony. They feed and care for the larvae.

Ants may be small insects, but queens can be big! They live far longer than other ants and have wings for part of their life.

Ant larvae, or grubs, don't have legs. They rely on adult ants to bring food and move them out of harm's way.

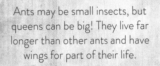

Fungus farmers

Leaf-cutter ants live in tropical forests and can be spotted carrying large pieces of leaf into their nests. They don't eat the leaves—instead they chew them up and wait for a forest of fungus to grow! They even "weed" these indoor gardens by removing unfriendly microbes.

Sweet treat

Lots of ants enjoy eating the honeydew produced by aphids. However, aphids are only alive at certain times of the year. Honeypot ants solve this problem by storing the sweet liquid in their bodies. When water and food is hard to find, workers stroke the bellies of the "honeypots" and they vomit up honey! It's so delicious, even humans like to snack on them!

Bristletails and silverfish

Insects lived on Earth long before humans—and even before dinosaurs. You'll find these "living fossils" hiding under stones, among dead leaves, and sometimes in our homes. If you spot one, take a closer look—it's like traveling back in time by 400 million years.

Bristletails dash from place to place looking for algae or lichens to nibble. If something frightens them, they can jump high into the air.

Living fossils

Bristletails and silverfish are almost identical to fossils of insects that lived almost 400 million years ago, so scientists can compare them to learn how other insects have evolved over time. For example, bristletails have a worse sense of smell than most insects, and their life cycles are simpler.

Bristletails

Order: Archaeognatha
Species: 500
Lives: in plant debris and under stones around the world

long palpi

long antennae

small head and eyes

scaly, cylinder-shaped body

Long filament and two cerci look like a bristly tail.

up to 0.7 in. long

By the sea

Shore bristletails can't swim, but they can jump out of the way of waves. This means they can live right beside the ocean, scraping algae (seaweed) off rocks to eat.

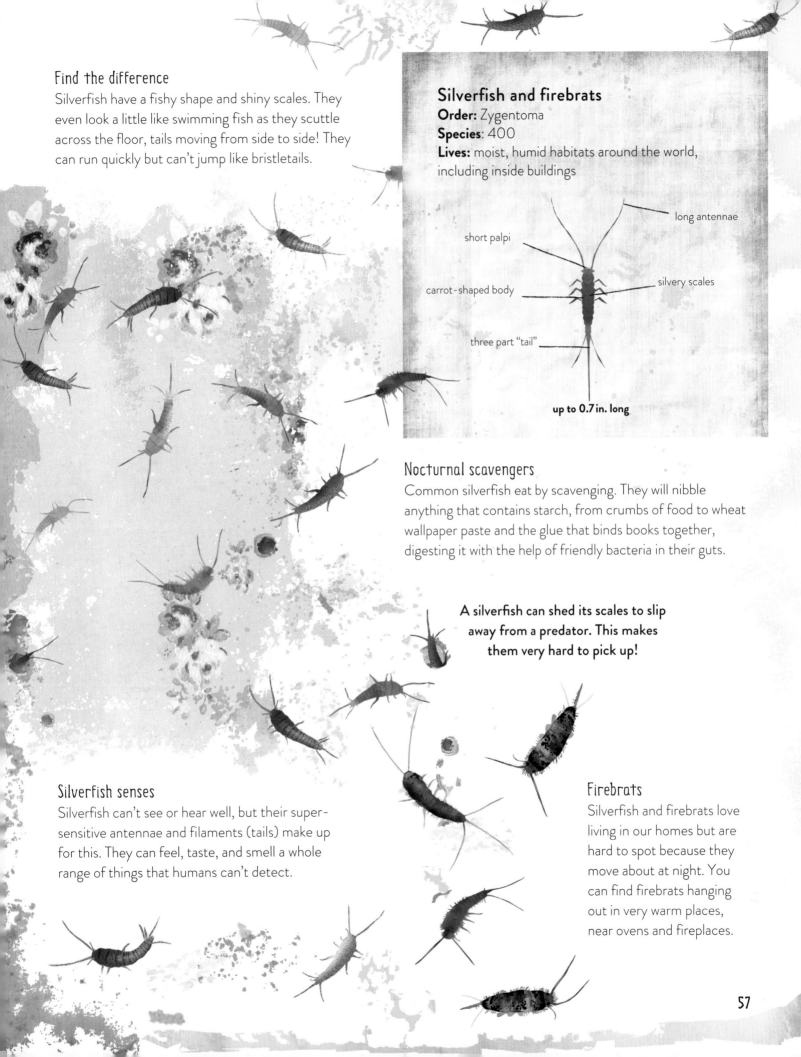

Find the difference

Silverfish have a fishy shape and shiny scales. They even look a little like swimming fish as they scuttle across the floor, tails moving from side to side! They can run quickly but can't jump like bristletails.

Silverfish and firebrats

Order: Zygentoma
Species: 400
Lives: moist, humid habitats around the world, including inside buildings

long antennae

short palpi

carrot-shaped body

silvery scales

three part "tail"

up to 0.7 in. long

Nocturnal scavengers

Common silverfish eat by scavenging. They will nibble anything that contains starch, from crumbs of food to wheat wallpaper paste and the glue that binds books together, digesting it with the help of friendly bacteria in their guts.

A silverfish can shed its scales to slip away from a predator. This makes them very hard to pick up!

Silverfish senses

Silverfish can't see or hear well, but their super-sensitive antennae and filaments (tails) make up for this. They can feel, taste, and smell a whole range of things that humans can't detect.

Firebrats

Silverfish and firebrats love living in our homes but are hard to spot because they move about at night. You can find firebrats hanging out in very warm places, near ovens and fireplaces.

Mayflies, dragonflies, and damselflies

Mayflies and dragonflies were among the very first insects with wings. They have been zooming and fluttering around Earth's fresh waterways for at least 300 million years, meaning that they shared the skies with pterodactyls and pterosaurs!

Mayflies

Order: Ephemeroptera
Species: 3,100
Lives: around the world, near fresh water

- no mouthparts
- large eyes
- large, triangular front wings
- short antennae
- small hind wings
- long cerci and filaments

up to 4 in. long

Super swarms

The adult mayflies only have a few hours or days left to live. An built-in clock means that millions of mayflies become adults at the same time, forming huge swarms. This gives them the best chance of finding a mate in a short space of time. Their fertilized eggs drop into the water, and the cycle starts again.

Mayfly nymphs

Most of a mayfly's life is spent as a nymph in rivers and streams, where it feeds on algae and plants for up to two years. Mayfly nymphs are easily harmed by water pollution, so lots of mayflies is a sign of clean water and a healthy ecosystem.

Madagascan mayfly nymphs grow so big they look more like crustaceans!

Teenage stage

Mayflies are the only insect with a "teenage" life stage! After wriggling out of their nymph skin for the last time, these young adults fly up out of the water and find a safe place to molt into real adults, ready to mate.

Perfect predators

Three hundred million years of evolution have fine-tuned dragonflies into perfect predators, which catch 95 percent of the prey they attack. Incredible eyesight and flying skills help them grab prey in midair with their front legs.

Living helicopters

Dragonflies are such great aerial acrobats that they inspire drone designers! Their front and back wings can beat at different angles and speeds, allowing dragonflies to fly backward, vertically, and upside down. However, they rely on sunshine to warm up their muscles, so you'll only see dragonflies dive-bombing prey (and each other) on sunny days.

Extraordinary eyes

A dragonfly's head is almost entirely eye. Thirty thousand different lenses allow the dragonfly to focus on details above, below, and almost all the way around its body. Human eyes can detect three colors of light—red, green, and blue. Dragonfly eyes can detect at least 11 different colors, including ultraviolet.

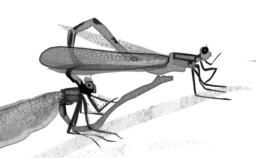

Forming hearts

Pairs of damselflies form a wheel or heart shape as they mate. Grabbing cerci help them stay together even as they fly.

Globe skimmer dragonflies migrate further than any other insect, flying up to 11,200 mi. every year.

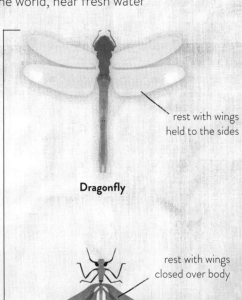

Dragonflies and damselflies

Order: Odonata
Species: 5,600
Lives: around the world, near fresh water

biting mouthparts

large eyes

four long, narrow wings

long body

spiny legs

cerci

rest with wings held to the sides

Dragonfly

rest with wings closed over body

Damselfly

up to 4.7 in. long

Millions more

Around a million species of insects have been spotted and named so far. There may be millions more to discover, but they are disappearing faster than we can find them.

Over the past 400 million years, insects have outlived dinosaurs, outlasted ice ages, and outperformed much larger animals. However, we may now be in the middle of a mass extinction that insects can't outsmart. A growing human population has put the planet under pressure. Natural habitats have been polluted or even destroyed. Climates are changing. Almost half of insect species are falling in numbers. Insects are dying out eight times faster than mammals, birds, and reptiles. The most endangered insects are moths, butterflies, ants, bees, wasps, and beetles.

Fantastic new insect species and superpowers are discovered every year. In Borneo strange yellow goo ants have been discovered whose workers defend their nest by exploding when disturbed! Scientists discovered that wax moth caterpillars can digest plastic, with the help of microbes in their guts. You can even have a species named after you. A treehopper species (*Hebetica sylviae*) was named after two-year-old Sylvie who discovered it in her backyard.

Protect insects!

There are so many reasons to protect insects. The biggest is because they are part of the incredible biodiversity on planet Earth. They are important to almost every other living thing on the planet—providing food, recycling nutrients, and pollinating plants (including most of the plants we eat). Without insects, ecosystems will collapse.

Every insect counts! And insects are everywhere! They are our bizarre, beautiful, wonderful neighbors—and we need each other more than ever. Next time you spot an insect scuttling in a forest, scurrying around your home, or fluttering about a garden, ask yourself what you can do to help protect the most important creatures on our planet.

What can you do?

Dig a mini pond

Make places for insects to hide

Leave "weeds" and grass to grow

Make a compost pile

Plant wildflowers

Never use chemicals outdoors

Glossary

abdomen: the bulb-like part of an insect's body that contains the digestive system and the reproductive organs.

antennae (singular: antenna): the pair of "feelers" attached to the head of an arthropod, used for sensing.

arachnid: a class of arthropods that have eight legs and no antennae, inlcuding spiders, ticks, scorpions, and mites.

arthropod: an invertebrate, such as a spider or insect, that has an exoskeleton, a segmented body, and jointed appendages (legs).

biodiversity: the variety of life that can be found on Earth, such as plants, insects, and animals, and the habitats they live in and the groups they form.

bioluminescence: the light produced (and emitted) by chemical reactions in living organisms, such as fireflies or glowworms.

camouflage: the colors and patterns of an insect or animal's skin that help it blend in (hide) with its environment.

carnivore: a meat eater; a creature that eats other creatures.

cerci (singular: cercus): the sensory appendages at the end of the abdomen of some insects and other arthropods.

chrysalis: the hardened outer layer of a pupa that protects it while it grows and changes into its adult stage.

decomposer: tiny organisms, such as bacteria or fungi, that break down dead or decaying matter.

ecosystem: a group of living organisms that live and interact with each other in a specific environment.

elytra (singular: elytron): the hard front wings of beetles and some other insects which cover and protect the hind wings underneath.

exoskeleton: the hard outer skeleton of many invertebrates, such as insects.

habitat: the natural home of an animal, insect, or plant (all organisms). A habitat meets all the conditions environmentally that an organism needs to survive.

halteres: a pair of short projections or modified wings in some insects that are used for maintaining balance during flight.

invertebrate: an animal or insect with no backbone.

iridescent: having a display of shimmering colors that seem to change when seen from different angles.

larvae (singular: larva): the second stage of life of an insect, between the egg and the adult stage.

mandibles: the two parts of an insect's mouth which it uses for biting.

metamorphosis: a change of form, such as that from a caterpillar to a butterfly.

microbe (or microorganism): a tiny organism, such as a bacterium or fungus, that can only be seen under a microscope.

mimic: to copy or look like. For example, an insect might copy the behavior of another insect or have similar coloring or patterns on its body to protect itself from predators.

molting: the way in which insects cast off or shed part of their body—usually an outer layer or covering, at specific points in their life cycle.

nymph: the young form of some invertebrates, particularly insects, which undergoes changes (metamorphosis) before reaching its adult stage.

order (scientific): all life on Earth is categorized and organized into groups to help distinguish how similar or different living organisms are to each other. There are eight major levels of classification: domain, kingdom, phylum, class, order, family, genus and species. The order category is made up of families sharing a set of similar characteristics.

organism: a living creature such as a plant, animal, or insect, consisting of one or more cells.

ovipositor: the tube-like egg-laying organ of most female insects.

palpi (singular: palpus): the sensory appendages attached to the mouthparts of insects.

parasite: an organism that lives on or in another organism (its host) and feeds off its host, often until the host dies.

pollination: a part of the life cycle of plants in which insects, birds, other animals, and the wind take pollen from one flowering plant to another of the same species. This allows the plants to produce seeds and reproduce (make new plants).

predator: an animal or insect that hunts (preys on) other animals or insects.

prey: an animal or insect that is hunted or eaten by another animal or insect.

proboscis: the long, tube-like mouth of some insects, used for sucking up their food.

pupa: the stage of development of an insect between a larva and a fully grown adult.

reproduction: the biological process by which new individual organisms (offspring) are produced from their parents.

resilin: an elastic-like protein found in insects and other arthropods that helps them jump or pivot their wings.

species: a group of organisms that have many characteristics in common and can only breed with each other.

spiracle: an external opening used for breathing. They are usually situated on the sides of an insect's thorax and its abdomen.

thorax: one of the three body parts of an insect. The thorax is the middle section between the head and the abdomen. The legs and wings are attached to the thorax.

toxic: poisonous

translucent: semitransparent

tymbal: an exoskeletal structure used to produce sounds in insects.

Index